North Shore

Poems of Mourning and Remembrance

David Caplan

Teaneck, New Jersey

NORTH SHORE © 2025 David Caplan. All rights reserved. No part of this book may be used or reproduced in any manner whatsoever without written permission except in the case of brief quotations embodied in critical articles and reviews.

Published by Ben Yehuda Press
122 Ayers Court #1B
Teaneck, NJ 07666

http://www.BenYehudaPress.com

To subscribe to our monthly book club and support independent Jewish publishing, visit
https://www.patreon.com/BenYehudaPress

Jewish Poetry Project #47   http://jpoetry.us

978-1-963475-49-4 pb

Cover illustration: "Sun is Shinning" by Drica Lobo.

Library of Congress Cataloging-in-Publication Data

Names: Caplan, David, 1969- author
Title: North Shore : poems of mourning and remembrance / David Caplan.
Description: Teaneck, New Jersey : Ben Yehuda Press, [2025] | Series: The
  Jewish Poetry Project ; 47 | Summary: "A deeply personal and reflective
  collection that explores the loss of the poet's father through the lens
  of Jewish tradition, memory, and everyday moments"-- Provided by
  publisher.
Identifiers: LCCN 2025005441 | ISBN 9781963475494 paperback
Subjects: LCSH: Jews--United States--Poetry | Fathers--Death--Poetry |
  Fathers and sons--Poetry | Grief--Poetry | LCGFT: Biographical poetry
Classification: LCC PS3603.A66 N67 2025 | DDC 811/.6--dc23/eng/20250414
LC record available at https://lccn.loc.gov/2025005441

25 26 27 / 10 9 8 7 6 5 4 3 2   20250415

For my father,
Edward Caplan לברכה זכרונו
and my mother,
Diana Caplan,
for the selfless care and devoted love
she showed him during his last years

Contents

I

Kitchen / 2
Mornings Like This / 3

II

My Father Playing Cards / 6
The Patriots or the Red Sox / 7
Inheritance / 8
Another Old Joke / 9
The Ride Home with the Radio On / 10
Best of Boston / 11
Teaching Hospital / 12
Speed Chess in the Fens / 13
Pray for What You Need / 14

III

After the Storm / 16
Sailing Lessons / 18
Bronze Pineapple / 19
Pizzeria / 20
Salemite / 21
Directions / 22
Rocky Road / 23
Pantoum at Dusk / 24
The Rat / 25

IV

Psalm / 28
Winthrop / 29
Each Grief / 30
My Father's Suit / 31
Border Collies / 32
Tom Brady / 33
Comforting a Mourner / 34
Last Joke / 35

V

Little Cheat / 38
Three Days / 39
Halftime / 40
It Didn't Take Much / 41
New Hampshire / 42
Accounts Payable, Accounts Receivable / 43
Fenway / 44
My Father's Shoulders / 45
No One Leaves This World / 46
Mass Ave / 47
Lost Time / 48
No One Should Grieve to Excess / 49
Souls Must Exist / 50
Some in Light, Some in Shade / 51
Notes / 52
About the Author / 55

I

Kitchen

When my mother asked him, "Do you know who this is?"
my father turned his head to find the right angle.
Pointing, she said the first sound in my name.

All those years I could not wait to get away.
"David, David," my mother repeated,
drawing out the two syllables like a spell,

and the ripped-out back wall returned to the kitchen,
the tall cabinets that I could not reach as a boy.
A blue ceramic bowl dried upside down beside the sink.

*If I am I because you are you, and you are you
because I am I, then I am not I and you are not you*,
a great mystic taught his students.

But isn't it always true of fathers and sons,
I am I because you are you, even after the father
does not recognize his son and the son realizes

everything in life is learned too late?

Mornings Like This

It was one of the tricks my mother learned.
She hired a contractor to expand the bathroom
with a shower big enough for her and my father

because he needed her there, to clean him,
her voice, the only one he recognized,
repeating, *It's okay*, when he grabbed her wrist.

What does she think on mornings like this,
showering inside that big space, responsible
only to herself? *It's okay*, she said,

sometimes a question, sometimes a plea,
like the prayers I was taught as a boy,
not knowing what they meant.

II

My Father Playing Cards

If you want to know friendship, watch them play poker.
Watch them deal cards, pass bowls of pretzels and salty chips,
and retell jokes too old for this century,

like that one about the rabbi, sick of it all, retired to Florida.
On Yom Kippur he goes golfing.
"Hashem, how can you let this happen?" all the angels protest,
"Why not smite him with a downpour, maybe some well-placed
   lightning?"

"Enough," Hashem tells them so what can they do?
The angels shut up. The rabbi strides to the first tee, no wait time at all,
stretches his stiff back and quads, and addresses the ball,
and the angels are getting ready to start squawking again
about sin and ingratitude, so Hashem says, "Not one more word,"
but then the rabbi playing golf on Yom Kippur hits a hole in one.
The angels go wild, howling about the desecration, the violation

of the holiest day of the year by a heretic in a pom pom tartan flat cap,
who should be in synagogue, beating his chest, bowing, and fasting,
not stuffing his face with a hotdog topped high with sauerkraut,
and hitting a hole in one on a postcard day with no clouds,
and Hashem, showing why he is Hashem, infinitely wise and just,
asks the protesting angels, "So who is he going to tell?"

Watch the men laugh because they know that having a story
and not being able to share it is the worst punishment of all,
a circle of laughing men who could have told the joke themselves,
and watch my father add a little imitation chortle,
a crooked little *ha ha*, laughing because they are laughing,
still recognizing that sound, and one of my father's friends
turns his cards over for him and tells him he has won.

The Patriots or the Red Sox

The father cut my father's hair, the son, mine.
How kindly they talked to him about the Patriots
or the Red Sox, depending on the season,
so he could enjoy the familiar sound of men discussing sports,
before the clippers returned to their work.

Let me praise how they held a mirror
to the back of his head so he could see how cleanly
the razor had sculptured his neckline.
They asked for his approval and pretended he gave it,

the hair still perfect two weeks later,
brushed back from his face by the hospice nurse
before she gave him a shave and adjusted the morphine.

Inheritance

How much of life is inherited?
My father's walk is my walk, the same
short stride testing the ground,

the same self-questioning shoulders,
but I did not inherit his kindness or his patience,
all those years he commuted into the city,

the car inching toward the tunnel,
stopping every few seconds, waiting.
Uncomplaining too about the diagnosis,

It just went away, he'd say about the end
of the sentence he'd started and wave
his hand like a gull in flight.

Another Old Joke

We all could use a joke. So how about this one?
A Catholic and a Protestant are arguing about when life begins.
The Catholic says conception, the Protestant, birth.

They are getting nowhere, nowhere at all, and friendships
have been lost over less. So they ask the old Jew
sunning himself on the next bench, "Moishe, who's right?"

And since old Jews in old Jewish jokes are always wise,
let's hear what he has to say: *When does life begin?*
That's easy. Life begins when the kids move out.

Old joke, right you are, right again with your sly
evasions and omissions. Right to ask when life begins
and not when it ends, with the death of the mind

or the death of the heart, right to leave
that question to us as we wait outside and three
nurses hold down my father so they can clean him.

The Ride Home with the Radio On

Up the onramp, the bridge arced from the city,
and two players who retired when I was a boy
retold the game we just watched, praising

a good shot sacrificed for a better one,
a pass spun exactly to where it needed to go.
They sounded ancient, but that was the point:

the game already its story, the shared surprise
of what happened and what didn't,
the feint, the quick back cut, and reverse layup,

and the defender, cunningly turned the wrong direction,
berating a teammate for his own mistake.
All games believe they never will end,

that's what we need them to do, believe
that we can make it last as long as we want,
the ride home with the radio on, my father

still well enough to pretend he is listening
to the old champions explain what we saw.

Best of Boston

Two flights of beer gleam against their marble trays.
My brother and I listen to the waiter

explain how each glass will taste. The pale ales
gleam as if backlit, porter, pilsner, and stout,

their acidity and strength, their liveliness,
and although we promised each other

we wouldn't talk about our father tonight,
each glass adds another pleasure taken from him,

only our mother feeding him something sweet,
cooing, "Good, good."

Teaching Hospital

How many years of research are heard
when the neurologist asks my father the date,

how many years of training in the protocols of patience
when he and his resident wait just long enough

for my father not to feel rushed, but all
that research and all that training only add

to the sadness of watching my father know
that he should know how to answer the doctor's question.

When his eyes return to my mother for help,
each of us calculates how close we are to him

not answering the few questions he still can:
where his nose is, his eyes, my mother's name, his name.

Each of us calculates the date when the next
consolation will be taken away.

Speed Chess in the Fens

"That's right, our souls are trash,"
          the street preacher shouts when a garbage truck
stops at the red light, and everyone laughs,

even the preacher, everyone except the chess
          players moving their pieces so quickly
they must know what will happen next,

like Olmsted surveying the saltwater marsh,
          knowing where the strollers will go,
the shade my father and I follow.

Again, he asks me where we are.
          The father mistaken for the son,
the son, the father, both of us wait

for the right answer, one he will remember.

Pray for What You Need

Twenty-five hours into the fast, twilight
hurries across the town green and steeples,
hurries to this little synagogue by the Atlantic.

Pray for what you need, the rabbi said.
So that's what I did. I prayed for an ordinary day,
for my father to wake early, shower, shave, dress himself,

and ask my mother where today's *Globe* is,
startling her dozing in the chair beside his bed.
A curse into a blessing, isn't that what we call it?

I prayed for what I needed: for the unfairness
of a kind man dying cruelly to be rectified
and my parents return to their lives,

tease each other and laugh no different now
than sixty years ago when my father arrived
for a date a little too proud of his new blazer and tie

and my mother scooped a pile of raked leaves
and dumped it over his head.

III

After the Storm

I

My brother and I considered the trawlers
the Atlantic had beached past the Fish House
as if it had forgotten it was supposed to stop

before the seawall's useless warning, the high line tide
redefined as low, the street a new harbor.
Both of us certain it would soon be fixed, the lattice

clematis returned to each spring beside the cut-through,
the salt air withdrawing behind us, the shower
where we washed away that smell before we headed inside.

II

                Who wouldn't want a month off school?
Sledding the country club's highest hill—no Jews were members,
  everyone knew—we raced to see how far we could make it last:

  trespassers owning the white hill spiked with ice.

David Caplan

III

After the storm, the town moved closer to the Atlantic,
cupolas raised to views past Egg Rock, past the confusions of broken
lobsterpots and buoys, new streetlights curved to look old.

If only neurofibrillary tangles were no different than power lines,
saltwater and seaweed pumped from basements,
then my father and I could talk about that spring,

how he lifted me onto his shoulders so I could see how smoothly
masons sprayed concrete against the gashed seawall.

Sailing Lessons

Slowly then suddenly, that's how it happens:
the widgeon topples

and they dive into another season,
autumn already in the gray open water.

They've come to practice capsizing,
zigzagging like a story through the harbor.

The keel slippery as a tongue,
treading water, they pull until the boat rights.

The weakest boy goes last, the others,
a colony of gulls, cawing encouragement—

is that why he takes a little longer?
Shivering in his lifejacket,

he knows their friendship is no more real
than the shipwreck

and fumbles with the keel to make it last.

Bronze Pineapple

Note the bronze pineapple beside the doorway,
the promise of hospitality and safe return,
and the marker naming the first owners

and their professions: *mariner, merchant, deacon.*
Walk in any direction and you will see streets
repeat those names like a teacher taking roll.

Twice daily, the incoming tide reviews the lesson.
No gutturals to soften, no hesitation, only
the nonchalance of moored boats aligned by the wind,

the launch that ferries members back to shore.
Biking the causeway home, even then we knew
we would never be loved back, no matter

how long we'd live here, how well we learned
the clapboard homes and old patriots' mansions,
the gossip of wood siding scored to look like stone.

Pizzeria

Lanky and white aproned like a robin,
he spun the pizza dough one-handed
tossing it on the downbeat—

better than any advertisement, any garish
outline of a slice, the dough,
an orb set into orbit, a perfect "O,"
the long syllable that lengthens a good surprise.

Most of all, we loved his nonchalance,
how he never once acknowledged us
outside the pizzeria's big front window,
leaning against our bikes, trying not to look
awestruck at our first experience of style.

Salemite

Down Derby Street, past the Custom House,
I lifted dumbbells until I felt how I wanted to look.
My arms twice their size, the long mirror approved each vein.

Leg days, I swayed down the gym's stairs into the October fog,
enjoying the soreness, that promise of self-punishment.
Another quiz on Monday, twenty more pages of Hawthorne's Puritans.

Ninth grade, no one knew what to make of them,
their weird speeches and obsessions, stern and black browed
like wiccans reading tarots cards for tourists.

The new inhabitant has little claim to be called a Salemite,
that I understood. Wasn't that what each swastika taught,
scrawled in schoolbooks for us to find?

Directions

If you want to give me directions I can follow,
don't mention street names or addresses, only
the names of the families who lived here last century,

the twin brothers I played catch with barehand,
extravagantly freckled and skinny, daring me
to throw the baseball harder.

Mention the town's monuments and cul-de-sacs,
its low stone walls, skeletons of the original estates,
and the abandoned railroad tracks I'd cut through,

imagining the great sound it must have made,
that churning of arrival and departure.
If you want me to follow, orient me in memory, not fact.

Rocky Road

Evenings long as summers, lingering in ice cream parlors,
between bites of rocky road or blueberry pie, we talked
about what else? the boredom of our small town by the beach,
its slow time, last summer's song forever on the radio,
pleading *Don't you forget about me*, and the certain knowledge
that excitement was elsewhere, but where, we weren't sure,
although we wanted nothing more than to rid our lives
of that boredom, our fathers home at 6:15 in time for dinner,
sports on the local news, the smirking broadcaster asking,
Why can't we get guys like that? whenever a traded player
hit a homerun and of course we thought of ourselves,
the boredom of our bodies that wouldn't run quite fast enough
or throw a ball with enough precision to be sent away and missed.

Pantoum at Dusk

Whatever it touches trembles.
The day's last swimmers hide as shadows.
Some sparklers burn, a few clouds pass,
And flashlights wave the traffic home.

The day's last swimmers hide as shadows.
The pier is empty, fathers whisper,
And flashlights wave the traffic home.
Frail shooting stars race up the hill.

The pier is empty except for whispers
And children swaying for a kiss.
Frail shooting stars race up the hill.
The bay's small boats turn on their lights

And sway like children for a kiss.
There is a room not far away.
The bay's small boats turn on their lights.
The sand is wet with last night's rain.

Yes, there's a room not far away.
Let sparklers burn, let all clouds pass.
The sand is wet with last night's rain.
Whatever it touches trembles.

The Rat

What's the point in being ironic about it?
The first time I heard feedback bouncing off
the back wall of that basement club,

the anarchy of untuned guitars hobnailed
with a fury that couldn't last —
what's the point of mocking what I felt?

Beauty is so rare a thing, but the right kind
of ugliness is rarer, and that's what we wanted,
Rathskeller shortened to Rat and when the band

took their time backstage, we chanted
their words back to them, *Hey, ho, let's go*,
until it was loud enough for them to start,

each song the same, the same three chords
racing like breakers to end and start and again.

IV

Psalm

I have loved Him because He hears my voice,
some translate the first line of the psalm
I read in my father's hospice room.

Others understand the Hebrew to mean:
I would love Him if He would hear my voice
or *I wished that God would hear my voice.*

Because or *if*, *loved* or *wished*. Too tired to pick,
I listen to the morphine work on his cough.
Just past the window, another blue jay raids

the perfectly squared shrub, feasts, then darts off.

Winthrop

A mourner remembers the wrong things.
His timing is always bad. When the funeral
director asked if my father had a middle name,

I almost said, *Winthrop*, the name of the town
where my father lived with an aunt.
Twelve, he needed to learn the prayers

and the Torah portion for his bar mitzvah.
Maybe my grandfather, a widower, just needed him
out of the house. Wrecking the tune,

my father barely made it through the first prayer.
The cantor hired to teach him told him to try again.
A large man, broad as his desk.

When my father warbled, *He sustains the living
with loving kindness*, the cantor leaned forward,
raising his arm, and my father braced himself.

Instead of a fist, an upturned palm swayed
like a baton. *Maxwell*, my brother said,
and the funeral director wrote it down.

Each Grief

Each grief is different. Watch the two brothers
saying kaddish, swaying beside each other,

repeating the same words
just a little differently, inflecting

each with their own sadness and regret.

My Father's Suit

I wore my father's suit to his funeral,
tore the lapel and his white shirt,
three inches across the heart, repeating

what I was told to repeat: *Blessed is the true judge.*
The jacket curled into itself, the shirt turned gray,
and I could not recognize the cousin who shook

my hand and said something about loss and comfort,
the schedule of their commandments.
I couldn't hear what he said, couldn't recognize

the words and the meanings those sounds made.
Only the rocky soil did not blur, the raspy cut
the shovel made when I swung it back for more.

Border Collies

My mother tells me the town hired border collies
to chase away the Canadian geese.

Better than a shotgun, a few hours of charging and retreat,
and the fat birds no one likes fled the commons and its little pond,

but a mourner's grief is not like that: it cannot be chased off,
voted for or against, rezoned and sold.

When I go for a walk, it invites itself along.
When I go for a drive, it tells me to turn hours out of my way.

Tom Brady

They shook my hand and kissed me between bites of cold cuts
and coffeecake and talked about the new casino and Tom Brady
and told me my father's memory should be for a blessing and asked

if I knew the joke about the rabbi who decides that life is too short
not to try non-kosher food at least once. And if he going to sin,
why not go all the way? The rabbi heads to Le Grand Chichi Maison

and orders a whole pig, no appetizers, no side dishes, just straight swine.
You know what happens next. The president of the synagogue
and his wife walk into Le Grand Chichi Maison

and are seated at the table next to their rabbi's, just as the waiter
brings over a big silver tray and, with a grand flourish, raises the lid
and the rabbi looks down at a whole pig with an apple in its mouth

looking up at him and he can feel the synagogue president and his wife
look at him with the same pained, astonished expression,
their wrinkled lips puckered just like the pig's, and the rabbi

puffs himself up to his full height—five seven on a good day—
and bawls at the waiter, *What kind of restaurant is this?*
I order a baked apple and this is what you bring me!

Laughing we lean a little close and repeat
our favorite line so we can hear it again.
Hoarse from too much talking, who can say it best,

And this is what you bring me! make the false promise
sound almost convincing, that the right brazenness
can overcome whatever life brings?

Comforting a Mourner

Let's not pretend they kept the traditional laws of comforting a mourner,
the wisdom learned from the mistakes that Job's friends made,
the ancients who said the wrong things when they should have sat in silence

and let their presence console him. They did what they knew:
what helped and what didn't when they mourned their own losses.
The first of seven days, of thirty, then a year, that's what I needed:

jokes and stories, the indecorous roar of life everywhere in the house.

Last Joke

With a little prayer book telling me what to say and when,
I practice the afternoon prayers so I can lead them
and try not to think of the strangers preparing my father for burial,

the buckets of water they pour on him,
careful to expose only what needs to be exposed.
I repeat each prayer until it is hard

to hear the years of not praying and the years
when I just mumbled the words, barely caring
what they meant, and I realize

I must look like the old Jew in the joke,
talking to himself, talking in little bursts,
then holding up his hand, palm out, and going silent.

Finally someone asks, "Friend, are you okay?"
"You know how it is," he says.
"I am telling myself some jokes to cheer myself up."

"So why do you keep raising your hand?" "Oh, that's
to let me know not to bother because I heard that joke before."
Yes, that's how it is: we say these words again and again,

to ourselves and others, sometimes to pass the time,
sometimes to cheer ourselves up or hide our embarrassment,
sometimes because we want to help those we failed

during their lifetimes, hoping it is not too late.

V

Little Cheat

                I sway to make it lighter,
a little cheat to lift the barbell off my chest,

raise the heaviness I feel everywhere on me:
a month busy with the business of mourning,

low chairs and little sleep, a month out of time.
Tell me whom should I ask, who can tell me

how long it will take until it won't feel like a betrayal,
an ordinary afternoon's little complaints and pleasures,

the shower that lets my body no longer smell like a body,
all that warmth, falling as water, rising as steam?

Three Days

Nothing is harder for the soul than its separation
from the body, the mystics explain. For three days,
confused, the soul hovers, thinking it can return

to the cortege stopped at a red light
because the other cars won't give way,
past the town line, left at the rotary,

where my father and I watched the last shoe factory burn.
The whole block caved in like those old faces,
all bone and sadness, hustled into the hiss

of water firefighters sprayed on the tenements,
their hoses stretched to the harbor. Isn't memory like that,
like the soul newly separated from the body

staying where it can do so little, trying
to make sense of the petty slights of life
and the misery soaked into floors, waiting to ignite?

Wrapped in a blanket, an old woman complained,
It was cold and I was afraid. All I had was a nightdress.
I didn't want to go so fast, but they made me.

Halftime

Perfect in his satin team jacket and cocked fedora,
the man sweeping the parquet floor at halftime

snapped his broom whenever he turned so precisely
I asked my father how much of his job he enjoyed,

but he looked at me as I'd made some kind of mistake,
as the team jogged back to the court,

back to the championship banners they'd won.
My father hesitated because he was kind

and didn't want me to know, not yet,
the difference between a drive to the city for a game

and the drive to another workday's obligations,
another accounting of what had been bought and sold,

that needed to be balanced and made right.

It Didn't Take Much

It didn't take much, just two entrees cut in half,
something between them that she would have made
but with a different spice or sauce.

That happiness cannot be explained,
how much my parents liked to know what they would get
from the daily specials' subtle variations

chalked in cursive. It belongs to another century
like the slice of cheesecake they took home, tin foiled like a swan,
in time to watch Johnny Carson hold an envelope

to his turbaned head and divine the joke sealed inside.

New Hampshire

My father always kept a fifty behind the pictures in his wallet,
folded neatly so no one could see it, set aside just in case.
I bet my mother found it, when she went through his things.

How much of his life was like that, little sums set aside,
not just the thirty-year mortgage he paid off early,
the receipts he always checked against his bank statement?

Once, hours into a bike ride, my mother realized they could cross
into New Hampshire if they followed the coast a quarter mile farther.
So that's what they did, stopping just past the state sign,

the two of them stopping to enjoy their luck,
that coincidence of geography and timing, before they headed home.

Accounts Payable, Accounts Receivable

What did my father think about, swimming laps before work?
The route he should take, city streets or expressway?
Or did he think about the day's obligations, the quarterly

accounts payable and accounts receivable, the truths they told?
Good water today, boys, isn't that what one of the other swimmers
always said, a lawyer slim as a coxswain, joking because

it was always the same, the same enormous dim lights,
the lanes lined like punch cards so no one would drift?
Or did my father think about something else,

something private between him and my mother, or something
even she wouldn't have known, that he let himself imagine,
turned sideways as if he were still in bed, reaching and kicking?

Fenway

My father opened his mouth and smiled
as best as he could, my brother's arm reassuring him,
their backs to the perfect green field,
so a stranger could take their picture,
both of them knowing he would not be back.

My Father's Shoulders

Tailored to my father's shoulders, another blazer almost fits.
Everything feels like that, cut to a body almost mine:
a closetful of wingtips and loafers, suits to be given away.

My mother tells me to try on something else. A drawer opens
to collar stays for oxfords already folded into garbage bags
and an old watch I never saw him wear, a small gold rectangle.

When I wind it, it works for no more than a moment.
No reason to see what it will take to have it repaired,
with its missing second hand, split crystal, and who knows

what else broken inside, no reason except for my father's name
engraved on the back and the need to make something right,
no matter how small and inconsequential, no matter how late.

No One Leaves This World

No one leaves this world
with even half his desires fulfilled.
Was that true, then, of my father?

The back gate doorstopped with a brick,
held open by the right weight,
what regrets did he take

past the harbor's empty moorings,
the Atlantic collapsed into the sky?
At the beach where my parents met,

the pier ends before the dock.
When I was girl, my mother told me,
you could swim as far as you like.

No lifeguard would blow a whistle.
No adult would make you come back.

Mass Ave

No boy can imagine his father as a boy.
No boy can imagine his father his size,

but this bridge frat brothers measured
in the lengths of their shortest pledge

lets me remember my father at my age now,
driving the only car he bought for pleasure,

a two-seater with the top down even in late fall,
past the dog track and gas tanks, rowers

working the Charles to foam.

Lost Time

If you lived here, you'd be home now,
the billboard taunted him, stopped before the bridge.

Helicopters circled like a boss
so their pilots could count the lost time.

Sunlight for work, darkness for home—
two girls share a cigarette at Wonderland,

daydreaming as the outbound train turns toward the city.

No One Should Grieve to Excess

No one should grieve to excess, a mourner is told.
*Three days for weeping, seven for lamenting,
and thirty for abstaining from laundered clothes
and cutting the hair, no more,*
but I remember my father turning
where a policeman waved, another block,
another detour, the northbound traffic
forced south because the city took
whatever it needed to bury its expressways.
That summer, thousands of rats rioted,
sewer gray and ravenous.
Waiters beat them back with brooms.

Souls Must Exist

Because a mourner changes places in synagogue,
I move a few seats closer to the window
and watch the Atlantic double back,

like the prayers we repeat, morning, afternoon, and night.
Souls must exist. Otherwise, life would be too hard.
After my father died, the two of us alone

in the hospice room, I asked him to forgive me
for all the times I failed him. I could barely
say it but needed him to hear and forgive me,

my mother waiting in the hallway to be driven home,
the mirrors not yet covered in sheets,
our pictures on the table, his face mine, mine, his.

Some in Light, Some in Shade

On my father's third yahrzeit

A *mistake,* my neighbor called the flowerbed
where he planted the rhododendrons. I watched him
dig them up and replant them closer to the street.

Some do better in light, some in shade. That's all they needed,
cosexual, stamen and stem, purple marbled with lilac,
suspended like Venetian chandeliers above the dirt.

All summer walkers stopped to envy them.
They never missed a day, those walkers with their little dogs.
They checked their progress on their watches. They counted each step.

There are two kinds of knowledge, I learned in yeshiva.
The first is incremental. It adds to what you already know.
To gain the second, you must give up who you are.

All winter I waited for it to happen. When I prayed,
I prayed to enter the words I whispered.
Stunned by an early frost, the shrubs greyed overnight.

I can almost feel it on mornings like this, feel
how each of us, brittle as pollen, temporary as ice,
will rise from the body's last regret, just as the walkers

disregard the forecast and shiver into mist.

Notes

"Kitchen" quotes a teaching by the Chassidic rabbi, Menachem Mendel Morgensztern of Kotzk, most commonly known as the Kotzker Rebbe.

"My Father Playing Cards" is dedicated to Neil Cooper, Ron Gilefsky, Herb Goldberg, Harry Epstein, Bobbie Kaplan, Neil Cooper, Ed Smith, and Lou Weinstein.

"Salemite" partially quotes a passage from *The Scarlet Letter*, the novel the speaker has been assigned in school. The full passage is:

> The new inhabitant—who came himself from a foreign land, or whose father or grandfather came—has little claim to be called a Salemite; he has no conception of the oyster-like tenacity with which an old settler, over whom his third century is creeping, clings to the spot where his successive generations have been imbedded.

The opening lines of "No One Leaves This World" quotes *Kohelet Rabbah*, a rabbinical commentary on *Ecclesiastes*.

The opening lines of "No One Should Grieve to Excess" quotes the Code of Jewish Law, Shulchan Arukh, Yoreh De'ah, written by Rabbi Yosef Karo.

I would like to thank Julia Knobloch for carefully editing *North Shore*. The book is better for her thoughtful suggestions and insights. Thanks also to Larry Yudelson at Ben Yehuda Press, Alicia Ostriker, who commented on several poems, and Mag Gabbert, for our many conversations about poetry and poetry writing. I started this book as a faculty member of Ohio Wesleyan University and finished it as a faculty member at Southern Methodist University. I would like to thank my former colleagues at Ohio Wesleyan University, in particular Amy Butcher and Bob Olmstead, and all colleagues at Southern Methodist University for welcoming me so warmly to the university community. My greatest thanks must go to Ana M. Echevarria-Morales, for too many reasons to list, and Yehoshua November, for his friendship and many discussions about poetry and chassidus.

Poems in this book appeared in the following journals (sometimes in slightly different form): "No One Leaves This World," "Pray for What You Need," and "Souls Must Exist" in *Pleiades*, "Mornings Like This" in *Literary Matters*, "Accounts Payable, Accounts Receivable" in *Formes Poétiques Contemporaines*, and "Pray for What You Need" in *Lubavitch International*. I would like to thank the editors Michel Delville, Jenny Molberg, Baila Olidort, Alexis Sears, and Ryan Wilson.

About the Author

David Caplan is a poet, scholar, and literary critic. He previously published two poetry collections, *In the World He Created According to His Will* (University of Georgia Press) and *Into My Garden* (Ben Yehuda Press), as well as several monographs and critical studies. His honors include the *Virginia Quarterly Review*'s Emily Clark Balch Prize for Poetry, an Individual Excellence Award in Criticism from the Ohio Arts Council, and two Fulbright Lectureships in American Literature. He serves as the Daisy Deane Frensley Chair in English Literature at Southern Methodist University.

The Jewish Poetry Project

jpoetry.us

Ben Yehuda Press

From the Coffee House of Jewish Dreamers: Poems of Wonder and Wandering and the Weekly Torah Portion by Isidore Century

"Isidore Century is a wonderful poet. His poems are funny, deeply observed, without pretension." —*The Jewish Week*

The House at the Center of the World: Poetic Midrash on Sacred Space by Abe Mezrich

"Direct and accessible, Mezrich's midrashic poems often tease profound meaning out of his chosen Torah texts. These poems remind us that our Creator is forgiving, that the spiritual and physical can inform one another, and that the supernatural can be carried into the everyday."
—Yehoshua November, author of *God's Optimism*

we who desire: Poems and Torah riffs by Sue Swartz

"Sue Swartz does magnificent acrobatics with the Torah. She takes the English that's become staid and boring, and adds something that's new and strange and exciting. These are poems that leave a taste in your mouth, and you walk away from them thinking, what did I just read? Oh, yeah. It's the Bible."
—Matthue Roth, author, *Yom Kippur A Go-Go*

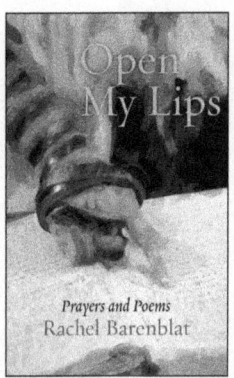

Open My Lips: Prayers and Poems by Rachel Barenblat

"Barenblat's God is a personal God—one who lets her cry on His shoulder, and who rocks her like a colicky baby. These poems bridge the gap between the ineffable and the human. This collection will bring comfort to those with a religion of their own, as well as those seeking a relationship with some kind of higher power."
—Satya Robyn, author, *The Most Beautiful Thing*

Words for Blessing the World: Poems in Hebrew and English by Herbert J. Levine

"These writings express a profoundly earth-based theology in a language that is clear and comprehensible. These are works to study and learn from."
—Rodger Kamenetz, author, *The Jew in the Lotus*

Shiva Moon: Poems by Maxine Silverman

"The poems, deeply felt, are spare, spoken in a quiet but compelling voice, as if we were listening in to her inner life. This book is a precious record of the transformation saying Kaddish can bring. It deserves to be read."
—Howard Schwartz, author, *The Library of Dreams*

is: heretical Jewish blessings and poems by Yaakov Moshe (Jay Michaelson)

"Finally, Torah that speaks to and through the lives we are actually living: expanding the tent of holiness to embrace what has been cast out, elevating what has been kept down, advancing what has been held back, reveling in questions, revealing contradictions."
—Eden Pearlstein, aka eprhyme

Texts to the Holy: Poems
by Rachel Barenblat

"These poems are remarkable, radiating a love of God that is full bodied, innocent, raw, pulsating, hot, drunk. I can hardly fathom their faith but am grateful for the vistas they open. I will sit with them, and invite you to do the same."
—Merle Feld, author of A Spiritual Life.

The Sabbath Bee: Love Songs to Shabbat
by Wilhelmina Gottschalk

"Torah, say our sages, has seventy faces. As these prose poems reveal, so too does Shabbat. Here we meet Shabbat as familiar housemate, as the child whose presence transforms a family, as a spreading tree, as an annoying friend who insists on being celebrated, as a woman, as a man, as a bee, as the ocean."
—Rachel Barenblat, author, *The Velveteen Rabbi's Haggadah*

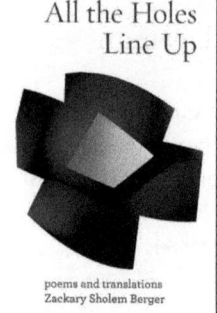

All the Holes Line Up: Poems and Translations
by Zackary Sholem Berger

"Spare and precise, Berger's poems gaze unflinchingly at—but also celebrate—human imperfection in its many forms. And what a delight that Berger also includes in this collection a handful of his resonant translations of some of the great Yiddish poets."
—Yehoshua November, author of *God's Optimism* and *Two World Exist*

How to Bless the New Moon:
Songs of the Sovereign and the Icon
by Rachel Kann

"Rachel Kann is a master wordsmith. Her poems are rich in content, packed with life's wisdom and imbued with soul. May this collection of her work enable more of the world to enjoy her offerings."
—Sarah Yehudit Schneider, author of *You Are What You Hate*

Into My Garden: Prayers
by David Caplan

"The beauty of Caplan's book is that it is not polemical. It does not set out to win an argument or ask you whether you've put your tefillin on today. These gentle poems invite the reader into one person's profound, ambiguous religious experience."
—*The Jewish Review of Books*

Between the Mountain and the Land is the Lesson: Poetic Midrash on Sacred Community by Abe Mezrich

"Abe Mezrich cuts straight back to the roots of the Midrashic tradition, sermonizing as a poet, rather than ideologue. Best of all, Abe knows how to ask questions and avoid the obvious answers."
—Jake Marmer, author, *Jazz Talmud*

NOKADDISH: Poems in the Void
by Hanoch Guy Kaner

"A subversive, midrashic play with meanings–specifically Jewish meanings, and then the reversal and negation of these meanings."
—Robert G. Margolis

An Added Soul: Poems for a New Old Religion
by Herbert J. Levine

"Herbert J. Levine's lovely poems swing wide the double doors of English and Hebrew and open on the awe of being. Clear and direct, at ease in both tongues, these lyrics embrace a holiness unyoked from myth and theistic searching."
—Lynn Levin, author, *The Minor Virtues*

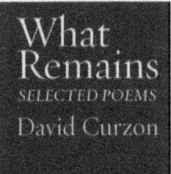

What Remains
by David Curzon

"Aphoristic, ekphrastic, and precise revelations animate WHAT REMAINS. In his stunning rewriting of Psalm 1 and other biblical passages, Curzon shows himself to be a fabricator, a collector, and an heir to the literature, arts, and wisdom traditions of the planet."
—Alicia Ostriker, author of *The Volcano and After*

The Shortest Skirt in Shul
by Sass Oron

"These poems exuberantly explore gender, Torah, the masks we wear, and the way our bodies (and the ways we wear them) at once threaten stable narratives, and offer the kind of liberation that saves our lives."
—Alicia Jo Rabins, author of *Divinity School*, composer of *Girls In Trouble*

Walking Triptychs
by Ilya Gutner

These are poems from when I walked about Shanghai and thought about the meaning of the Holocaust.

Book of Failed Salvation
by Julia Knobloch

"These beautiful poems express a tender longing for spiritual, physical, and emotional connection. They detail a life in movement—across distances, faith, love, and doubt."
—David Caplan, author, *Into My Garden*

Daily Blessings: Poems on Tractate Berakhot
by Hillel Broder

"Hillel Broder does not just write poetry about the Talmud; he also draws out the Talmud's poetry, finding lyricism amidst legality and re-setting the Talmud's rich images like precious gems in end-stopped lines of verse."
—Ilana Kurshan, author of *If All the Seas Were Ink*

The Red Door: A dark fairy tale told in poems
by Shawn C. Harris

"THE RED DOOR, like its poet author Shawn C. Harris, transcends genres and identities. It is an exploration in crossing worlds. It brings together poetry and story telling, imagery and life events, spirit and body, the real and the fantastic, Jewish past and Jewish present, to spin one tale." —Einat Wilf, author, *The War of Return*

The Missing Jew: Poems 1976-2022
by Rodger Kamenetz

"How does Rodger Kamenetz manage to have so singular a voice and at the same time precisely encapsulate the world view of an entire generation (also mine) of text-hungry American Jews born in the middle of the twentieth century?"
—Jacqueline Osherow, author, *Ultimatum from Paradise* and *My Lookalike at the Krishna Temple: Poems*

The Matter of Families
by Robert H. Deluty

"Robert Deluty's career-spanning collection of New and Selected poems captures the essence of his work: the power of love, joy, and connection, all tied together with the poet's glorious sense of humor. This book is Deluty's masterpiece."
—Richard M. Berlin, M.D., author of *Freud on My Couch*

There Is No Place Without You
by Maya Bernstein

"Bernstein's poems brim with energy and sound, moving the reader around a world mapped by motherhood, contemplation, religion, and the effects of illness on the body and spirit. Her language is lyrical, delicate, and poised; her lens is lucid and original."
—Anthony Anaxagorou, author of *After the Formalities*

Torah Limericks
by Rhonda Rosenheck

"Rhonda Rosenheck knows the Hebrew Bible, and she knows that it can stand up to the sometimes silly, sometimes snarky, but always insightful scholarship packed into each one of these interpretive jewels."
—Rabbi Hillel Norry

Words for a Dazzling Firmament
by Abe Mezrich

"Mezrich is a cultivated craftsman: interpretively astute, sonically deliberate, and spiritually cunning."

—Zohar Atkins, author of *Nineveh*

Everything Thaws
by R. B. Lemberg

"Full of glacier-sharp truths, and moments revealed between words like bodies beneath melting permafrost. As it becomes increasingly plain how deeply our world is shaped by war and climate change and grief and anger, articulating that shape feels urgent and necessary."
—Ruthanna Emrys, author of *A Half-Built Garden*

Ode to the Dove: *An illustrated, bilingual edition of a Yiddish poem by Abraham Sutzkever*
Zackary Sholem Berger, translator
Liora Ostroff, Illustrator

"An elegant volume for lovers of poetry."
—Justin Cammy, translator of *Sutzkever, From the Vilna Ghetto to Nuremberg: Memoir and Testimony*

Poems for a Cartoon Mouse
by Andrew Burt

"Andrew Burt's poetry magnifies the vanishingly small line between danger and safety. This collection asks whether order is an illusion that veils chaos, or vice-versa, juxtaposing images from the Bible with animated films."
—Ari Shapiro, host of NPR's *All Things Considered*

Old Shul
by Pinny Bulman

"Nostalgia gives way to a tender theology, a softly chuckling illumination from within the heart of/as a beautiful, broken sanctuary, somehow both gritty and fragile, grimy and iridescent – not unlike faith itself."
—Jake Marmer, author of *Cosmic Diaspora*

Feet In L.A., But My Womb Lives In Jerusalem, My Breath In Vermont
by Lori Levy

"Takes my breath away. With no pretense whatsoever, they leap, alive, from the page until this reader felt as if she were living Levy's life. How does the author do it?"
—Mary Jo Balistreri, author of *Still*

www.ingramcontent.com/pod-product-compliance
Lightning Source LLC
LaVergne TN
LVHW041346080426
835512LV00006B/643